We Can Play Percussion

Traditional songs for young children

We Can Play Percussion

Traditional songs for young children

kevin mayhew

We hope you enjoy the music in this book.
Further copies of this and our many other books are available
from your local Kevin Mayhew stockist.

In case of difficulty, or to request a catalogue,
please contact the publisher direct by writing to:

The Sales Department
KEVIN MAYHEW LTD
Buxhall
Stowmarket
Suffolk IP14 3BW

Phone 01449 737978
Fax 01449 737834
E-mail info@kevinmayhewltd.com

First published in Great Britain in 2003 by Kevin Mayhew Ltd.

© Copyright 2003 Kevin Mayhew Ltd.

ISBN 1 84417 088 8
ISMN M 57024 204 7
Catalogue No: 3611746

0 1 2 3 4 5 6 7 8 9

The music in this book is protected by copyright and may not be reproduced
in any way for sale or private use without the consent of the copyright owner.

Cover design: Patrick Baker
Music setter: Donald Thomson
Proof reader: Marian Hellen

Printed and bound in Great Britain

Contents

	Page	Track
Five Little Ducks	12	2
If You're Happy and You Know It	10	1
Little Peter Rabbit	22	7
O, We Can Play	20	6
Penny on the Water	16	4
Ten Fat Sausages	18	5
The Bear Went Over the Mountain	28	10
Tommy Thumb	14	3
When I Was One	26	9
Wind the Bobbin Up	24	8

Introduction

These songs have been scored for the following instruments: claves, an egg-shaker, a jingle stick, maracas, small drum (tambour) and a triangle. These instruments are all included in the Kevin Mayhew Children's Percussion Set. Of course, these parts may be freely adapted for other percussion instruments. Here are some suggestions for playing the instruments, not only to have fun but also to help children develop an awareness of the basic musical elements: tempo, timbre, dynamics, duration and . . . silence!

Getting to know the instruments

Encourage children to experiment with percussion instruments. Let them have fun and discover many different ways to produce a whole variety of sounds. If there is a group of children, let them share their discoveries and try to imitate each other's ideas. Perhaps limit children to one instrument at a time so that they really explore the sound possibilities of one instrument before rushing on to the next. Make it all very 'hands on' and make plenty of noise!

Claves

Hold a clave in each hand and strike one with the other. Note how the sound differs depending how tightly you grip the claves. Holding both fairly loosely gives the most resonant sound.

Egg-shaker
Hold the egg in the palm of the hand and play with a gentle to-and-fro movement; towards you and away from you is better than side to side. Here again, notice how the sound changes as you tighten or loosen the grip.

Jingle stick
Shaking the stick with the jingles facing you, rather than sideways on, produces the best sound.

Maracas
The maracas are played holding one in each hand, but experiment with two at a time. Play a variety of rhythmic patterns with both hands playing the same rhythm or try some of the following simple patterns with the hands playing alternately: LRLR, RLRL, LLRL, RRLR, LRRL, RLLR.

Small drum
Holding the drum in one hand, the instrument may be played with the beater or the fingers of the other hand. Notice that the sound is different if you strike the centre rather than near the rim. Try the handle of the beater 'across' the rim of the drum or, to produce a trill, strike the drum by rotating the thumb and finger.

Triangle
Suspend the triangle from one hand and strike it with the beater held fairly loosely in the other. A trill can be produced by striking quickly across the 'closed' lower corner of the triangle.

Activities

Percussion instruments may be used in a variety of ways to foster the children's enjoyment; here are a few simple suggestions:

- Tell a story and play a different instrument to represent each character in the tale.
- Make sound pictures, e.g. the weather or a trip in a sailing boat.
- Play a rhythm and get the child to play it back.
- Try further elementary ear training by asking the children to cover their eyes and guess which instrument is being played.
- Ask the children to play the rhythm of their own name, school, town, favourite food or football team. It's fun playing the names in reverse, surname first!

Rhythmic patterns underpin every area of our lives from the beat of our hearts and the changing of the seasons to the tick of a clock and the drip of a tap. Little wonder then that a strong percussive pulse is found in so much of the world's music. We trust that these simple arrangements will encourage children to participate in the fun and excitement of making music.

Accompanying the play-along CD

The children will enjoy singing along to the CD and improvising their own percussion parts. For a more structured approach, two suggestions have been given for playing along and these have been used on the recording. For very young children, these simple ostinati may need further simplification.

1. Ostinato – using a short, repeated rhythmic pattern throughout the song.
2. Key Words – emphasising certain words or strong rhythmic patterns by playing on particular beats and breaking the ostinato at this point. Key Words are shown in the lyrics with capital letters.

Things to try
1. Where an ostinato uses more than one instrument, seat the children opposite each other; this may help to reinforce the pattern visually.
2. Use movement to reinforce the rhythm: e.g. in the song *The Bear Went Over the Mountain,* marching on the spot, two-to-the-bar, gives a 'moving along' feel; the instrument is played when the feet strike the floor.
3. Rather than play all the instruments in every song, choose instruments which complement the music: e.g. the triangle alone will give a gentle feel to *Penny on the Water.*

IF YOU'RE HAPPY AND YOU KNOW IT

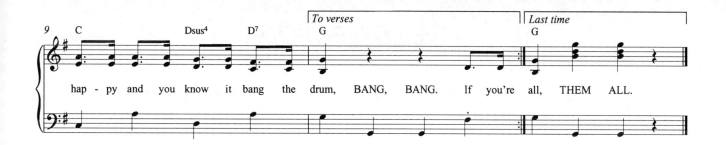

Other instruments play as indicated by the lyrics.

If you're happy and you know it shake the stick, SHAKE, SHAKE, *etc.*

If you're happy and you know it click the claves, CLICK, CLICK, *etc.*

If you're happy and you know it shake the egg, SHAKE, SHAKE, *etc.*

If you're happy and you know it play them all, THEM ALL, *etc.*

FIVE LITTLE DUCKS

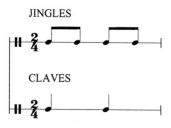

Four little ducks *etc.*

Three little ducks *etc.*

Two little ducks *etc.*

One little duck went swimming one day,
over the hills and far away.
Daddy Duck said, 'QUACK, QUACK, QUACK, QUACK,'
and five little ducks came swimming back.

TOMMY THUMB

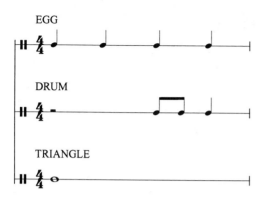

Peter Pointer's up and Peter Pointer's down, *etc.*

Toby Tall is up and Toby Tall is down, *etc.*

Ruby Ring is up and Ruby Ring is down, *etc.*

Baby Small is up and Baby Small is down, *etc.*

Fingers All are up and Fingers All are down, *etc.*

PENNY ON THE WATER

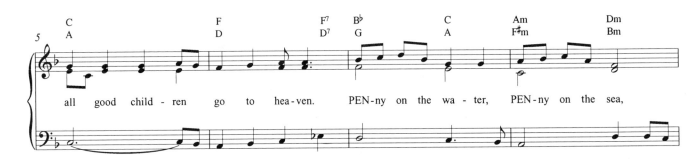

TRIANGLE

TEN FAT SAUSAGES

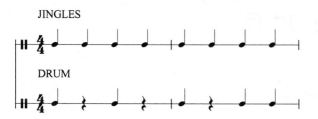

Eight fat sausages sizzling in a pan, *etc.*

Six fat sausages sizzling in a pan, *etc.*

Four fat sausages sizzling in a pan, *etc.*

Two fat sausages sizzling in a pan, *etc.*

O, WE CAN PLAY

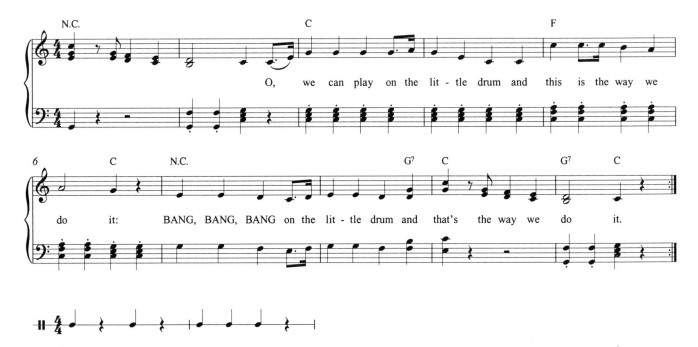

Play instruments as indicated by the lyrics

© Copyright 2003 Kevin Mayhew Ltd.
It is illegal to photocopy music.

O, we can play on the triangle . . .
TING, TING, TING on the triangle . . .

O, we can play on the jingle stick . . .
SHAKE, SHAKE, SHAKE on the jingle stick . . .

O, we can play on the maracas . . .
SHAKE, SHAKE, SHAKE on the maracas . . .

O, we can play on the wooden claves . . .
CLICK, CLICK, CLICK on the wooden claves . . .

O, we can play on the little egg . . .
SHAKE, SHAKE, SHAKE on the little egg . . .

O, we can play on the instruments . . .
PLAY, PLAY, PLAY on the instruments . . .

LITTLE PETER RABBIT

Little Peter Rabbit had a fly upon his paw, *etc.*

Little Peter Rabbit had a fly upon his tail, *etc.*

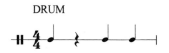

WIND it back again, WIND it back again,
PULL, PULL, CLAP, CLAP, CLAP. *rpt.*
POINT to the ceiling, POINT to the floor, *etc.*

WHEN I WAS ONE

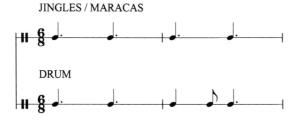

When I was two I buckled my shoe, *etc*.

When I was three I grazed my knee, *etc*.

When I was four I knocked on the door, *etc*.

When I was five I learned to dive, *etc*.

THE BEAR WENT OVER THE MOUNTAIN

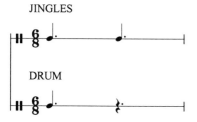